The Real Story of Us

The Real Story of Us: A Seven-Week Interactive Journey into Genesis 1-3

For information, visit www.metanoiatoday.com

ISBN: 979-8-9936501-0-4

Published in the United States

Edited by Kathy Brown.

Cover design and layout formatting based on a template created by Nelly Murariu at PixBeeDesign.com.

The Real Story of Us

A Seven-Week Interactive Journey into Genesis 1-3

Wendy Elzinga

To Tod, Cassidy, Jake, and Julia:
You are all well acquainted with my own brokenness and love me in spite of it! I love you all, too, more than words can say! May the work you've been given to do be a reflection of your gifts and talents and of your gratitude for your Creator's love for you and for a desperate world!

Contents

Author's Note

This Bible study may be a bit different from others you have read, as I am going to ask you to slowly read Genesis 1–3 before we begin. As you will soon see, it will set the stage for everything we need to understand about our existence, the core of our woundedness and where we are in the grand story of all things! We will refer to various other passages throughout the Bible as we go along. As you read, take notes and jot down any questions you may have. We may address some of those, but if we don't, please explore those questions in your group or on your own. Writing questions about the text as I read the Bible is one of my favorite ways to dig deeper, and I find it's a good way to build my relationship with God by asking Him questions as I go along.

When I ask God, "Why did you put that there?" or "What does that mean?", it's a form of prayer. I am talking to Him as a friend, almost as though we are sitting together as I read and He is stirring my curiosity, enticing me to grow in my understanding of who He is. Sometimes, something will be revealed quickly, and other times, those questions remain a mystery. But God wants us to keep digging, to keep pursuing more of Him. I have read these three chapters in Genesis repeatedly while preparing this study, asking questions and curiously exploring the text. Each time I read the passage, I discover something new. I recommend that you read the passage several times throughout the study. I believe these first three chapters of Genesis set the stage for everything that follows in the Bible and beyond, continuing to this present moment, in a way that helps us understand ourselves better.

As a therapist working with individuals and couples, I conceptualize a framework for the therapy process. I want people to KNOW, HEAL, and GROW. The knowing part is helping them understand the problem they bring to the sessions. This involves psychoeducation of the problem, helping them understand how their personal and family histories play a role and helping them gain self-awareness. It may involve teaching how the nervous system is wired to protect them or how their personality shapes their situation. We spend a lot of time understanding the factors that contribute to where they are now so that they can begin to HEAL as we work through traumas, relationship issues, emotional pain, and grief. Ultimately, they GROW by making meaning out of their life's circumstances, defining and living out of their values and uncovering and overcoming obstacles to become the best version of themselves. This process is meant to enable people to flourish individually, relationally, and spiritually.

I've found that it is important to KNOW "why"—why things are the way they are, why we are the way we are, and why other people are the way they are. Sure, we can go back to experiences we've had, such as patterns passed down from our family of origin and choices and habits we've developed throughout life. These things tell us a lot about ourselves. But essentially, the core issues we face find their origin in the Garden of Eden. Like it or not, as a result of the events that unfolded in that mysterious ancient place, we are now broken people; meaning an imperfect version of our former sinless state, living in challenging relationships with other broken people, existing in a broken world. And we have an enemy that is always trying to derail, deceive and defeat us, if not downright destroy our lives.

When we recognize that this first story of the Bible connects to who we are today and the problems we face, we can better put the circumstances of our lives into perspective. We can see the best solution to life's challenges lies in knowing, loving, and trusting in a God who has everything under His control, a Father who is always lovingly pursuing and redeeming us and healing that which is broken. He understands the mess we are in and He desires to bring us hope and healing in the midst of it all. Maybe we can't see any of that yet, but my prayer is that by the end of the study, you may start to glimpse that hope and reality.

How to get the most out of this study

This study is intended to be done individually or with a group. Some helpful strategies in each chapter can be used to apply what we've talked about. I call these strategies "Tools of the Trade," and I often teach them to my clients to help them achieve their goals. The questions at the end of each chapter can be used for group discussion or as prompts for reflective journaling. Also, I've included a prayer at the end of each chapter. Feel free to recite it or use it as a springboard to pray what's on your heart after reading the chapter.

You will notice some examples "From the Therapist's Office." These are fictionalized accounts based on compilations of many real people and issues that I have encountered after nearly twenty years as a therapist. I've tried to recreate the themes presented in therapy while disguising and keeping confidential any details about individuals so that no one can be identified. If anything sounds familiar, this has more to do with common prevalent topics than any one person's story.

A disclaimer: While I am a trained therapist and am offering you a glimpse into the therapist's office and some strategies I use with my clients, *I am not your therapist.* I realize that for some, the situations that drew you to this study may be heavy and difficult. I encourage anyone who is experiencing deep pain or struggling to cope with life's difficulties to seek help. Resources are available for those who feel there is no hope. If this applies to you, I urge you to contact the suicide hotline in the United States by simply dialing 988 to talk to someone who can help you navigate the crisis you are in. If you find that life is a struggle, I urge you to seek treatment from a mental health professional (see possible resources in the back of the study). As for spiritual guidance and support, please find a local church where you can connect and be surrounded by the love and prayer of others.

This book is designed to be a seven-week study if you read one chapter a week. This will give you time to reflect on the material and try the exercises included. Many book clubs and small groups meet weekly, so this is designed to fit with a group study. However, if you want to read it faster or slower, feel free to modify it. There is no one right way to do this study.

My biggest hope is that you come away with the understanding that, given our collective beginning, the difficulties of life may make more sense. And given what we can learn about God through His Word, we can be filled with hope that wherever we find ourselves, it is not yet the end of the story. We've been given the beginning and the end in God's Word, and though we now find ourselves in the middle—perhaps the chapter of greatest peril in our own lives, and maybe in the timeline of history—we are assured that He is working in and through it all, even now. We can hold onto the truth that the story has a very good ending.

Let's begin at the beginning! To start, read Genesis 1–3.

Chapter One

Why is Life So Difficult

The theme of this wild story for which we find ourselves

So, the Lord God banished him from the Garden of Eden to work the ground from which he had been taken. After he drove the man out, he placed on the east side of the Garden of Eden cherubim and a flaming sword flashing back and forth to guard the way to the tree of life.
Genesis 3:23-24 NIV

Chapter 1 Why is Life So Difficult

From the Therapists Office

Jamie sits slumped in the soft gray chair in my office, head in her hands, tearfully recounting the events of her difficult marriage. Things happened that she didn't expect. Marriage is hard, harder than she thought. She remembers a time when she felt hopeful and excited about the future with her new husband. But now, several years into the marriage, she recounts feeling let down by the promises of marital bliss. After a cross-country move she didn't want, as well as ongoing financial strain, she confesses she feels disconnected from the man she once fell in love with. She also misses her support system back home. Frustrated with repeated unresolved arguments with her husband, she feels hopeless and considers leaving the marriage in hopes of finding someone else. She longs for an opportunity to get it right the next time.

What About You?

That is Jamie's story. Your story may be different, but I would be willing to bet that you, too, have at times felt disillusioned by life as it has unfolded throughout the years.

Deep within us lies the belief that we were meant for something wonderful, to be happy and fulfilled, to have dreams that come true, and to enjoy rewarding relationships and work. But we find brokenness, heartache, confusion, and disappointment all around us. If you can't relate to this and haven't yet personally experienced any pain or sorrow in this life, I regret to inform you that eventually you will. In fact, everyone will face personal challenges, struggle, or pain to some degree within their lifetime.

You get it, though, right? Even if you haven't been personally touched (yet), you can see that something isn't quite the way it was meant to be. Something is off. What we know and desire in our hearts doesn't align with the reality we see around us, and it often doesn't fit with our own experiences.

The longing for things to be right and good versus the reality of living in a world that is not right is a tension we can't escape. However, that tension is often the very thing that compels us to pursue what we sense is missing—the good and right way that things should be. And though we may, at times, be misguided in our pursuit, this tension was meant to draw us to God Himself.

We will struggle to make sense of it all if we don't understand the unfolding story that we find ourselves in. This story goes back to the very beginning of creation. Like all good time-tested stories, it has a setting, characters, a crisis, a villain, and a hero. But this "story" happens to be true, and we each have our place in it. As we will soon find out, the events in the beginning of the story impact each and every one of us to this very day.

Every day, all around the world, there are people struggling with a life-changing trauma, a scary diagnosis, a betrayal by a spouse, an unexpected job loss, or the sudden death of a loved one. Life is filled with grief, fear, frustration, and confusion. Furthermore, the things we might rely on such as wealth, power, and fame do not protect any one of us from pain or death.

If we have a good God who is in control of all things, why would He allow such tragedies to exist? Not all my clients believe in God, and I'm always curious about how people develop their beliefs, so I'll ask more about this. This is what I often hear: "A good God would not allow me or others to experience such suffering without intervening." The conclusion for many is that He either doesn't exist or isn't good.

In order to reconcile the trials and heartache we see around us with the fact that we do have a good and loving God who is in control of all things, we need to journey back to the beginning—the first chapter of the big story we all exist within. With that as the backdrop, we will understand how our lives have been affected by our enemy, our own brokenness, the brokenness of others, and the challenge of living in a broken world made of broken systems.

But we will not be left in despair. Please know that there is hope. Hope is found within the overarching theme of the drama we find ourselves in, and hope exists in our individual stories as well.

When we recognize the story as it plays out in our own lives, we can begin to adjust our own expectations. Sometimes our pain is exacerbated by our own unmet longings. Life, we believe, is supposed to go as we planned: Our partner is supposed to meet all of our needs, for example, and our children should be appreciative of all we do. We don't often plan on accidents or illnesses or job losses, but they come. We don't often prepare ourselves for disappointments and frustrations. The world encourages our unrealistic expectations. Just a couple decades ago, we saw perfect lives portrayed on television, and we may have been envious or sensed our longing, but we could tell ourselves those perfect portrayals weren't real.

Today, we see people on social media living all kinds of dream lives, and we suddenly feel as if we've been conned. It seems, perhaps, that the dream life *is* possible after all, and our own life pales in comparison. We want "this couple's" marriage—they have so much fun and seem so much in love with each other. Or we desire "that woman's" easy work schedule—she works as she travels all over the world while still somehow raising and homeschooling seven of the most adorable children while maintaining a beautiful house and designer wardrobe. We feel inadequate, left out of some great cosmic reward system, and ashamed that we don't measure up.

Sometimes, like Jamie, we may be tempted to leave the life we've been given and start all over in pursuit of a life more deserving of us. Please remember as you notice all the exciting lives portrayed around you that people always put their best selves on display in public and hide what causes them shame or inadequacy. We will see that this behavior, too, has roots in the beginning. With a steady stream of content forever in the palm of our hand, we constantly see images of the elusive "good and perfect life" dangled before our eyes.

Friends, I've seen the destructive impact of social media—especially on younger generations who have never experienced life without the connected world of the internet. In some ways, all the beauty and happiness on display there can inspire us to be better versions of ourselves, but often, in reality, what we observe crushes us instead. I've witnessed a real spirit of emptiness and despair in my work as a therapist that often manifests in anxiety or depression. These may be accompanied by a constant comparison to others and internal dialogue centered around not being enough or not having enough, along with a twin fear of not measuring up to others' expectations of us. There is a real fear of being judged and found to be without worth or value in the eyes of other people. This impacts one's own sense of self-worth.

I wish people could allow the lens of reality to pan out and reveal a larger expanse of time and space to see that everyone suffers to some extent living in a broken world with broken people. Social media lets people curate an enviable life for the world to consume. But it still isn't the complete picture of reality. It's edited content of the really good stuff. Like those old television shows, the content stirs up a sense of inadequacy so that we feel compelled to do something or purchase something to feel better about our lives. The same advertisers that funded the television shows of perfect people living perfectly scripted lives now fund social media influencers. We live in a world system that is broken too. It depends on us feeling inadequate, unfulfilled, depressed, or anxious so that we are motivated to consume our way to fulfillment. But eventually, we generally come up feeling empty. This broken system can't offer us what we truly hunger for.

This desire for success and happiness isn't a bad thing! It isn't bad at all to desire good things. That is a quality of our God-image-bearing soul. We are meant to long for goodness, and that longing is meant to draw us closer to the giver of all good things, to remind us that our true home is not in this place. We have within us a forgotten, ancient memory of beauty and perfection once ours, now elusively out of reach. And I believe we possess an inner drive to go back to a time "when things were good." We may experience this as nostalgia, but I believe it is an ancient memory within each of us calling us to our true home.

We have a big problem, though: As a result of what we as Christians call "the fall," which began the moment our ancient parents ate the fruit of the tree of knowledge of good and evil, our desires and longing for the good life became bent and destructive. You see our existence would now be marked by experiencing within and around us the effects of both good and evil. We now exist in a world which juxtaposes pain and pleasure, loneliness and connection, life and death, joy and sadness. Ecclesiastes reminds us of this reality:

There is a time for everything, and a season for every activity under the heavens: a time to be born and a time to die, a time to plant and a time to uproot, a time to kill and a time to heal, a time to tear down and a time to build, a time to weep and a time to laugh ,a time to mourn and a time to dance, a time to scatter stones and a time to gather them, a time to embrace and a time to refrain from embracing, a time to search and a time to give up, a time to keep and a time to throw away, a time to tear and a time to mend, a time to be silent and a time to speak, a time to love and a time to hate, a time for war and a time for peace. Ecclesiastes 3:1-8

We've lost the perfect life we were made for and as a result we chase after things that are not beneficial to us. We want so badly for life to be only good that we have forgotten that the good life is only truly found in communion with the One who created us. Like our first parents, we are easily deceived. We need help, and there is good news: Help is available and our hero is calling us to it.

Tools of the Trade

Because our experience is marked by good and evil, we can intentionally focus on the good. Research points to the benefits of gratitude, so let me invite you to focus your attention on the positive things in your life right now. Intentionally focusing on blessings doesn't take away pain or sorrow, but it broadens our perspective. It can take us from a place of despair to a place of hope. We can start to see that maybe we *are* being looked out for and taken care

> ***"Every good and perfect gift is from above, coming down from the Father of the heavenly lights, who does not change like shifting shadows."* —James 1:17**

of. Maybe we can even start to see that we are cherished like the beloved children that we truly are. Ultimately, we can see and savor the rich blessings in our lives.

Because gratitude is so beneficial to our sense of well-being, I often ask my clients to keep a gratitude journal. Martin Seligman, a pioneer of positive psychology, teaches an exercise of writing down three good things each day for two weeks. In one study, participants rated themselves as happier after doing this assignment. This is because the brain is wired to overlook the positive things in our lives and to focus on the negative to promote survival. The brain is always scanning for problems that need to be solved or danger to be escaped. The more we focus on what we are grateful for and focus our attention on our blessings, the happier we are.

In another research study where a group of psychotherapy clients were asked to write letters of gratitude to others, those that did showed reduced symptoms of depression and anxiety compared to the control group that didn't write gratitude letters. When we focus on what is positive in our lives and those that contribute to it, our attention shifts away from the negative and we develop a greater sense of well-being.

I am going to suggest you try a modified version of these studies. Since we are directing our gratitude to God, begin to daily record three things that went well or name three good things in your life. Next, say a prayer of thankfulness for these blessings. Recording them will allow you to look back and see the faithfulness of God in your life.

Even if you are in the midst of a painful season of life, you can intentionally seek out blessing by writing down three things you are grateful for each day. This could be as simple as "I'm grateful for my warm, cozy socks," or "I'm grateful for coffee." Another suggestion is to notice your frustrations and turn them into gratitude. For example, try saying, "I am grateful for these beautiful children," even as you notice that they have forgotten to hang their coats up (and knowing that one day, those coats won't be there to bother you because your kids will have grown and flown).

Noticing and intentionally savoring the everyday experiences—as well as pausing to give thanks to the giver of all blessings—will do wonders for your perspective on life. If you struggle to find anything to be grateful for, can you be grateful for the incredible things your body can do? When my father-in-law slowly became paralyzed from a brain tumor, I remember the immense gratitude I felt in being able to move my body and require it do what I wanted it to do. I remember thinking how easily I had taken freedom of movement for granted.

Sometimes, with practice, people are even able to see the blessings that result from suffering or hardship. This can be hard, so don't worry if you are

> ***"And we know that for those who love God all things work together for good, for those who are called according to his purpose."* —Romans 8:28**

unable to do it. You don't have to feel guilty if you struggle to find something good in suffering. Just know that it can be possible to look at the difficulties in life and find redemptive meaning and purpose in them. It may take time to process all the emotions related to grief before you can start to find meaning in a difficult situation. Look for role models who have successfully redeemed suffering. Also, recognize that this is what God does. He redeems that which seems without hope.

Discussion Questions and Reflective Journaling Prompts

Do you ever get caught up in comparing your life to others? What emotions do you usually experience when you do this? Can you start to recognize that sometimes you are comparing yourself to only a "curated" part of someone else's life?

Think about a time you felt disillusioned with life—maybe when life didn't go as planned or perhaps when someone important let you down. Think of a time when real life didn't live up to your expectations. What happened? And how did it impact you?

Name some things you are currently grateful for

Prayer

Dear Lord,

I confess that I often focus on the pain and difficulties of my life, the things that are missing, but in doing so, I sometimes miss the blessings. Please help me to turn my attention to the beautiful blessings you have put in my life. Help me to experience gratefulness for the good things you've given to me and to see these things as a way You are pursuing my heart and drawing me closer to You, even in the midst of hard, heavy, or confusing circumstances. Help me to experience Your presence with me in the midst of my pain and suffering. Help me to know that You understand me and care about me as You, too, are familiar with suffering. Help me to be content even in the midst of any difficulty I am facing, knowing that my pain and suffering isn't the end of my story or Yours. Amen.

Chapter Two

Back to the Beginning

The original setting of the great story

God saw all that he had made, and it was very good.
Genesis 1:31 NIV

Chapter 2 Back to the Beginning

In the first two chapters of Genesis, we get a glimpse of the time in history when all was right and "very good" in the world. As we visit (or revisit) the beginning of the Bible, which describes the "genesis" of our world and history, we get a picture of God, who majestically and mysteriously created the whole universe by speaking it into existence. He was there before it all began.

Pause here for a moment to reflect on our God who has no beginning. Wow! It's hard to wrap your mind around that! He is a God of order and beauty and purpose, and His creation reflects this. God created man in His image; He created both males and females to be like Him—creative, kind, compassionate, intelligent, generous, witty, and wise, to name just a few qualities that separate humans from the rest of creation.

As we reflect on these chapters, we envision a place where God walked with humans in the garden and gave man the fulfilling work of stewardship, through naming and caring for the animals and cultivating the plants and trees. We will see that death didn't exist. God provided food through seed-bearing plants for both man and animals. Even the trees gifted their fruit without death. And certain trees held special powers. Eden was a magical, beautiful place where there was order and protection and everything was good. Humans didn't even have a need for clothing. There was nothing to be protected from, not even embarrassment or shame.

This was the world we were made for, a world that had everything we needed to thrive. Man lived harmoniously with creation and with each other, and God literally walked with us as a friend. Work was productive and enjoyable; fear and death had not entered the picture. There was no threat to safety (physical, psychological, emotional, or relational) in this place. Can you imagine it? No fear, no pain, no loss.

This is what Adam and Eve experienced before realizing they were naked. Before eating fruit from the tree of the knowledge of good and evil, it seems there was no shame, humiliation, or even vulnerability. That is where the *real* story of us began. And we have been struggling with vulnerability and fears of all kinds of threats ever since Adam and Eve fell into sin after being tempted by the serpent. They ate fruit from the tree God told them not to eat from.

Before this significant event at the very birth of human history, the world had never experienced death and was made up of living beings that existed harmoniously with each other. But even through the introduction of death (God sacrificed animals to provide coverings for Adam and Eve's nakedness and shame), a future redeemer is foreshadowed, one who would once and for all cover all shame through sacrificial death—a redeemer provided by God Himself. Adam and Eve tried to cover their shame themselves with fig leaves and were not able to adequately do so. God, from the very beginning, is letting us know that He alone is able to step in and bring us the hope we need.

As a result of living in a fallen world, our ecosystems and world systems are made up of predator and prey, vulnerability and death, and scarcity of resources. We live in a world of wild and untamable weather conditions. Our world experiences earthquakes, tornadoes, and hurricanes. Depending on where you live, you may have to contend with dangerous heat or cold, droughts or floods, landslides, avalanches, wildfires, damaging hail, and wind. There is no end to the weather conditions that can threaten life or sources of food. Poisonous plants, insects, and dangerous beasts abound. While most of us don't spend our days thinking about such things, we do have an awareness that our world isn't completely safe.

And we must be prepared for the threat of danger. Advances in science teach us much about how our brains and nervous systems are wired to identify and protect us from threat. I have often wondered if the human nervous system shifted and developed to protect us after the fall, when death and our severed attachment from God became a reality.

From the Therapist's Office

Ellen recounts her past week's success. She has been able to do her assignment—introduce herself to someone in her class and ask them a question about the lecture. She has not been able to do this before now. She struggles with social anxiety and feels that other people are judging her harshly. She believes she is not as smart or witty as others, and she imagines that they are always mocking her or laughing at her when she speaks. So, she shrinks publicly, becoming small and invisible. We talk about how her heart pounds and her hands shake and how she feels nauseous just thinking about talking to strangers. I've taught her to calm her nervous system by taking slow, deep breaths while reminding herself that she doesn't know nor can she control what other people think. Managing her breath is meant to keep her nervous system from reacting to threat.

We also have talked about recognizing that what people think about her—good or bad—does not define her, as people's thoughts are often more a reflection of themselves than the person they are thinking about. We've talked about tuning in to the fact that most other people want to be liked just as she does, and we've practiced noticing and responding to people who are warm and friendly. I've helped her practice allowing herself to notice and to experience the discomfort of her anxiety while managing her thoughts and behaviors as she imagines meeting people. Many people know how to do this instinctively, but Ellen views other people's thoughts as most likely negative. Therefore, her nervous system responds to others as if they are a threat and, in some way, dangerous. This has caused her to avoid and escape social interactions that she actually desperately needs in order to feel connected. The more she avoids and escapes, the lonelier she feels, and the stronger her fears become.

Nature and Our Nervous System

Therapists often help people to identify threats sometimes called triggers (real or imagined, current or from the past) that dysregulate the nervous system. Just like animals, humans are wired with survival mechanisms that help us scan our environment for threats and to fight, flee, or freeze to survive. This is the root of much of the anxiety people experience. Some people's "threat scanners" are particularly sensitive. This could be genetic, or it can result from previous experiences or traumas. People often tend to either become aggressive and fight their threats, or they flee by using escape and avoidance strategies. Sometimes people freeze, as if shutting down or putting up an invisible numbing wall between themselves and the threat. We are capable of seeing threats just about anywhere depending on our own experiences of real or perceived danger. Some people see threats in spiders or in closed-in spaces, for example.

We can also perceive threat from other people that is often related to our fear of their judgment, rejection, or abandonment of us, as in Ellen's case).

We were not made to live our lives in this state of constant alertness to threat. But as a result of the fall, many people have a deeply ingrained and persistent sense that they are no longer safe. And while it is true that our world is not the safe haven of Eden, we usually do not find ourselves in grave danger. However, our nervous systems may not always know that. For some people, the simple thought of letting down their guard and exposing vulnerability may feel threatening.

In the imperfect, not completely safe world we find ourselves in, God is still wooing us to Himself with the calming rhythms of his creation. We can still find a reflection of God who created all the beauty, order, and safety of Eden in our world today. When we immerse ourselves in nature, we can often experience a state of relaxation that turns off the threat signals within our nervous system. Even a creation marked with brokenness still demonstrates God's presence with us. We can experience that God remains in control. The seasons come and go in a consistent pattern. The sun and stars follow a steady course across the sky. Remarkable creativity is all around us, and wonder is found in the natural world that can leave us completely awestruck.

For many, contemplating their smallness in an incredibly complex universe can actually help regulate the nervous system that responds to the brain's signal of threat or safety. Think of gazing at the stars or a vast ocean. For me, it is helpful to remember that God still instructs the regular patterns of His creation. He pays attention to the smallest detail (even a sparrow doesn't fall without His care (see Matthew 10:29). He hasn't abandoned me, you, or His creation.

When my children were younger, we started to collect and raise monarch caterpillars. I still grow their food source, milkweed, and keep them in an enclosure where I give them fresh leaves daily to eat. Sometimes I find their tiny eggs, the size of a pencil point, on the leaves. Within two weeks, they are full-grown caterpillars ready to form a chrysalis. The caterpillar climbs to the top of the container, or branch, and sheds her striped skin. Underneath is the green chrysalis ringed in a circle of gold like a precious crown on top.

Her body then liquefies within the shell of the chrysalis, and for two more weeks, she is essentially dead. She is still and does not eat, but that liquid is forming a new body that looks completely different from the old body. She develops bright orange and black wings that can be seen through the translucent shell of the chrysalis right before she emerges as a new being. She goes from a creature that crawls on her belly to one who soars to the sky within two weeks' time. In fact, whenever I release a new butterfly, it soars right to the tops of the trees. What a contrast in perspective that must be. The former creature sees the world from a ground-level, limited viewpoint. The new one soars to the sky, transcending her former limits and seeing the world afresh from a broader vantage point. Things that were once so big must now look so small.

I tell you this because I think it reflects how God reveals something about His character through nature. Perhaps this is God telling us about Himself, about His story, and about how He makes all things new, how death isn't the end. Maybe He is reminding us that we can't see everything from where we are today. I believe that He is giving hints of Himself, His plans, and His character throughout creation. Even amid brokenness, He offers pictures of hope and new life.

Tools of the Trade

Recent research has also been showing us the healing impact of nature. Natural settings can calm and regulate our nervous systems. We are currently learning about the health benefits of exposure to green spaces (forests and gardens, for instance) and blue spaces (coastal environments, rivers, and lakes). People who not only spend time in nature but *interact* with it, for example, by intentionally immersing themselves in it and experiencing it with their five senses, have a greater sense of well-being. Their internal threat signals shut down and their relaxation response (the other part of the autonomic nervous system, known for helping us rest and repair) activates. We can experience the health benefits of nature by engaging in activities such as gardening, hiking, biking, fishing, boating or even just sitting on a park bench listening to and watching the birds.

One activity that can help you tune into nature is taking a mindful walk. You can do this if you feel that your surroundings are safe. When you do this walk, focus on observing what's around you. First, pay attention to how your feet feel as they hit the surface they are walking on. Next, tune in to what you see around you. Observe the variation in colors and textures and notice small changes in your surroundings. Notice the way the wind moves the grass or trees; notice any shadows or tiny insects crawling or flying around you.

Next, notice what you hear. Do you hear any wildlife? Birds singing? Squirrels scampering? Crickets chirping? Notice if you hear the wind rustling anything. Do you hear water, such as waves crashing, brooks bubbling, rain sprinkling, or kids splashing in a pool? Next, notice what you smell. Take a long, deep breath and notice the scents of any odors, dampness, or earthiness. Have you ever noticed the air smells different after a rainstorm or near the sea?

Finally, notice what you can feel, such as the temperature of the air, warm sand between your fingers, rough bark, or smooth stones. You can even taste something if you know it isn't poisonous. Notice your body's reaction to being in nature. Do you feel evidence of your relaxation response? Do you feel lighter, more relaxed, more curious, less stressed?

Not only does God reveal Himself through His creation but He also has made it for us, to nourish us, heal us, calm us, and remind us of Himself. His gentle rhythms laid out in nature were given to us to help us rest, relax, and tune out a world filled with stress and hurry, where the glaring and bright lights are all competing for our attention. Spending time in nature connects us to what we were made for. It can clear our minds, allowing God to reveal Himself and speak to us.

Discussion Questions and Reflective Journaling Prompts

How have you seen God displayed in His Creation?

How do you see Him whispering His story to you, drawing you to Him through what He has made?

If you tried the nature walk, tune in to your anxiety level beforehand. I use a 1 to10 rating scale, with 1 being very relaxed and 10 being the most anxious you have ever felt. Then rate your level after the nature walk. Since this is completely subjective, there is no right answer. This is just to help you pay attention to what your nervous system is communicating and maybe help you identify a coping skill to bring you more peace.

Prayer

Thank you, Lord, that you have placed me in a world that reflects You in so many ways, even in its broken state, we can see incredible beauty all around us. Help me to remember that I, too, reflect You even in my imperfect human nature. Give me opportunities to see Your glory through what You have made. Grant me the peace and awe that comes from being surrounded by the beauty of nature. Amen

Chapter Three

Meet Your Enemy

Your story has a villain

The Lord God took the man and put him in the Garden of Eden to work it and take care of it. And the Lord God commanded the man, "You are free to eat from any tree in the garden; but you must not eat from the tree of the knowledge of good and evil, for when you eat from it you will certainly die."
Genesis 2:15–1

Chapter 3 Meet Your Enemy

From the Therapist's Office

Jeff struggles with addiction to alcohol, though he doesn't completely admit that. He minimizes the problem and says he can stop drinking anytime. But he has had some struggles with work because of it. His family has confronted him about how his drinking has hurt them, embarrassed them, or made him unavailable to them. He thinks they are overreacting, but the truth is, he is afraid that if they are right, he will have to give up the one thing that makes life seem bearable. It's the one thing he's found that numbs the pain of feeling like a failure or feeling completely overwhelmed by life's demands. His thoughts tell him that he can't measure up to everyone's expectations. He feels the stresses in life are bigger than his capacity to handle them, and he feels the pressure to be perfect at all things.

Jeff believes that he has no one to depend on but himself. This is the first lie he believes. Then, internally, he hears a whisper telling him that he is inadequate, a failure. When the pain associated with those thoughts becomes unbearable, he entertains the thought of drinking to soothe the pain, to make it go away. As the alcohol delivers its numbing effects, he forms an agreement with the deceptive message that alcohol can take away the pain of all of his heavy emotions because the pattern he has developed seems to work in the moment. All this pain can disappear in the time it takes to drink a few servings of alcohol. Understanding from the Word of God how Satan operates, I firmly believe that Satan is deceiving Jeff by whispering these lies into his mind, and he is making an agreement with them and permitting them to become his own thoughts. These thoughts then become the root of the behaviors that spring from them.

Satan's Tactics

It is dangerous to believe that our enemy, Satan does not exists. When we deny his influence, we come to all kinds of faulty conclusions about why bad things happen. But when we recognize that Genesis introduces us to our enemy so that we understand how he operates, we can identify and refute his influence in our life. Remember he is sly. Some people believe they could easily recognize him and the schemes he utilizes to frighten or tempt us. The world paints a picture of Satan as dark and scary or silly and cartoonish. In reality, our adversary sidles up to us in the guise of a friend who only wants what's best for us. It's as if he has a deep understanding of us and knows our longings and our weaknesses inside and out. If he can disarm us with his persuasions, then he can guide us down a path that eventually destroys us. Here's how Satan appealed to Eve, as recorded in the passage below.

Now the serpent was more crafty than any of the wild animals the Lord God had made. He said to the woman, "Did God really say, 'You must not eat from any tree in the garden?" The woman said to the serpent, "We may eat fruit from the trees in the garden, but God did say, 'You must not eat fruit from the tree that is in the middle of the garden, and you must not touch it, or you will die.'" "You will not certainly die," the serpent said to the woman. "For God knows that when you eat from it your eyes will be opened, and you will be like God, knowing good and evil." When the woman saw that the fruit of the tree was good for food and pleasing to the eye, and also desirable for gaining wisdom, she took some and ate it. She also gave some to her husband, who was with her, and he ate it. Then the eyes of both of them were opened, and they realized they were naked: so, they sewed fig leaves together and made coverings for themselves.
Genesis 3:1-6

He coaxes us with desirable words and gets us to question truth. Notice the way he spoke to Eve. He started with questions that caused Eve to question what she knew. *Did God really say . . .?* If we start to question what God says, then we are easily confused about truth, and Satan has opened the door to deceive us.

Once he entices us in our thought life, Satan then continues to increasingly bind us like a prisoner to the consequences of the desire that started it all. James 1:13–15 provides a scary picture of how this can eventually play out: "When tempted, no one should say, 'God is tempting me.' For God cannot be tempted by evil, nor does he tempt anyone; but each person is tempted when they are dragged away by their own evil desire and enticed. Then, after desire has conceived, it gives birth to sin; and sin, when it is full-grown, gives birth to death."

We can see Satan's tactics when we compare how he tempts Eve in the Garden to how he tempts Jesus in the desert.

Satan appeals to our appetite. The appetite can be for anything—food, sex, power, wealth, control, or revenge, to name a few examples.

The Bible shows Satan tempting Eve's appetite for the forbidden fruit, pressing her to see that it is appealing, good for food, and good for obtaining wisdom and becoming like God.

In the New Testament, when Satan tempts Christ in the desert, he again goes for the appetite. He first tempts Jesus to turn stones into bread, as Jesus has been fasting for forty days and is hungry. Jesus rebukes him with Scripture, letting Satan know that He is fueled not by food alone but by the Word of God. I believe He is also demonstrating that there is spiritual power in fasting.

Satan tempts us to distrust that God's Word is true. His desire is that we will lose sight of God and of truth. He whispers, "Prove that God is who He says He is," and "Show me that God will do what He says he will do." By enticing us to question God, he lures us into disobedience.

He causes us to question whether God has good plans for us or even that God is good or that He is for us. He tempts us to test that God has the power, the ability, or even the concern to do what He says He will do.

He tries to convince us that God's boundaries were meant to deprive us and not protect us. He tries to convince us to take matters into our own hands. Eve is tempted to distrust the Word of God and to test God by eating the fruit to see if God is withholding something wonderful from her—the knowledge to be like Him. Likewise, Jesus is tempted to show His power, to prove He is who He says He is, that He is truly the Son of God.

Satan promises we can be like God. As the father of lies, Satan seduces Eve to trust his words over God's. He promises her she will have the same knowledge as God. He promises that Eve will not die. And in this lie, Satan is whispering that Eve can be independent of God, that she can live her own way. Of course, this is a trick and a deception. But Eve makes her choice. She distrusts God, trusts Satan, and takes the fruit to her own detriment and to the detriment of the human race. Once she eats the fruit, death enters into the world.

Satan tempts Jesus to bow to him and gain rule over everything, claiming he has been given some level of authority over the world and can give it to anyone he pleases.

Jesus understands that Satan has no power or authority apart from what God has allowed him to have, even if we struggle to make sense of how this works. Even theologians have differing views of Satan and how he operates. But ultimately, Jesus came to strip Satan of his power, knowing it will involve suffering and His own death. In the desert, Satan seems to be offering Jesus a way to bypass the immense cost and negotiate a deal.

Jesus is not deceived by Satan's tactics. He uses the authority of Scripture to refute Satan because He *is* the Word of God. He refuses to distrust or disobey the will of God by taking the (supposedly) easy road promised by Satan and sidestepping the sacrifice He must make to provide a way for us to have freedom from spiritual death. He shows us how to trust that God's ways and God's plan are good.

As for each one of us, Satan ultimately wants to destroy our relationship with God. He wants us to believe that God isn't for us. He wants us to believe God has forgotten us or is holding out on us, that we are not precious. He doesn't want us to recognize and use the power we have in Christ as His dearly loved children to resist him. Most people don't go out of their way looking to self-destruct. Most gamblers don't envision losing their lifelong savings and perhaps relationships. Most adulterers don't cheat seeking to destroy their family; most addicts don't foresee that they may lose jobs, homes, and family when they try their first substance. But we see it happen again and again as people are led down a path that initially seems far more pleasurable and rewarding than the dangerous snare that is waiting around the corner.

But Satan sees it. With a friendly "I'm on your side" approach, he coaxed Eve down a path of destruction. He knew she would die if she ate the fruit. He knew she and her husband would be banished from Eden. He knew he would damage something precious to God. He hid his true motives all too well as he persuaded Eve to "take a bite."

In all the ways that Eve failed (and let's not forget Adam, who was complicit in all of this. He ate the fruit Eve gave him), Jesus didn't fail. Adam and Eve's failure led to death and brokenness. Jesus, by refusing to give in to Satan's temptation, gave us the power and taught us how to resist it. It was the beginning of the end of Satan's power over us. Jesus's wilderness experience, where Satan tempted him, was followed by His public ministry and death on the cross. In this, Jesus fulfilled the promised curse God made to the serpent in Genesis 3:5: "And I will put enmity between you and the woman, and between your offspring and hers; he will crush your head, and you will strike his heel"

In removing our enemy's power to accuse us and hold our sin debts as evidence against us before God, Jesus provided a way for us to be reconciled with God, and He established His kingdom on Earth. It continues to grow to this day as people put their trust in Him and in His promise to make all things new.

So why is Satan still at work in this world? Why is he still able to ensnare people? Though we may not know the answers to these questions, we need to remember that we have been promised power over the influence of Satan through Jesus and the work of the Holy Spirit who has come to be our helper after the resurrection of Jesus. For those not familiar with

Christianity and even those that are, this can seem mysterious and complex. Let's break it down a bit.

Jesus died on the cross, taking on the punishment for our sins. He rose from the grave, giving us victory over sin and death, but He then left us for a while, letting us know He is preparing a place for us with Him. He promised to return, but meanwhile, we remain in vulnerable human bodies on a broken planet with broken people, living amid broken world systems. And we have an enemy who prowls around seeking to destroy us.

God does not want to leave us alone in this. He promises that we can overcome all this, and He gives us the means to do so. His kingdom is something we can be part of now, even with all the brokenness around us. When we confess our sinfulness (our brokenness) and make Jesus the Lord of our life, we belong to a new spiritual kingdom within a world that is wounded and suffering.

As a part of this spiritual kingdom, we have access to the Word of God, which is the very thing Jesus used to resist the temptation of the devil and what caused Satan to leave Him alone. He gives us a community of believers to strengthen and support us, and He gives us Himself in the form of the Holy Spirit. Consider the Spirit as an inner source of power and guidance that provides you the right words to say when facing any difficulty, that gives you a gut feeling or intuition about something, or that prompts you to do or say something. The Spirit is also a source of power to overcome temptation. The more time you spend in prayer and in the Word of God, the more you feed on what nourishes your spirit and strengthens you to recognize the voice of the Holy Spirit and draw from His power—the power that Jesus Himself accessed to defeat the enemy.

When Jesus refused to turn stones into bread in Matthew 4:4, He quoted words from the book of Deuteronomy: "Man does not live by bread alone but by every word that comes from God." He was reminding us that our spiritual nourishment and strength come from this spiritual food. Spending time studying Scripture and letting it comfort and guide you is good spiritual self-care. It's a spiritual diet that helps make you resilient to the troubles of this world.

Satan's Tactic	*Tempting Eve*	*Eve's Response*	*Tempting Jesus*	*Jesus's Response*
Appeal to appetite	"Take the fruit; it is good to eat."	Takes the fruit because it looks good for food.	"Turn the stones into bread."	*But Jesus answered him, saying, "It is written, 'Man shall not live by bread alone, but by every word of God.'"* — Matthew 4:4
Appeal to be like God (power, wisdom, authority)	Obtain ability to be like God in knowing good and evil.	Takes the fruit hoping to be like God, knowing good and evil.	Worship and serve Satan to obtain power over Satan's dominion.	*Jesus said to him, "Away from me, Satan! For it is written: 'Worship the Lord your God, and serve him only.'"* — Matthew 4:10
Distrust God's Word/His goodness. Test God by disobeying Him.	"You will not surely die."	Takes fruit to test God's Word—does He really mean what He says or is He withholding good things?	"Throw yourself down from this high place. God will send his angels to save you." (You will not surely die.)	*Jesus answered him, "It is also written: 'Do not put the Lord your God to the test.'"* — Matthew 4:7

Tools of the Trade

If we want to know an important way Satan works in our own lives, we need to pay attention to our thoughts. The apostle Paul worried that, like Eve, our minds would be led astray (see 2 Corinthians 11:3). Remember that the primary way Satan tempts us is by stirring our own appetites. He will convince us to do any number of things to satisfy our hunger for pleasure, power, or relief from pain, whether that is through food, sex, wealth, substances, or mindless movie binging. He tempts us and reminds us how good it will feel, how much we deserve it, and so forth. He tempts us to disbelieve or disregard God and to distrust God's goodness by testing Him. He appeals to our vanity, our longing for pleasure, our sense of fairness, and our desire to be in charge of our own lives. And as Eve has shown us, he leads us to destruction.

People don't often ponder their internal dialogue to develop an awareness of how their thoughts impact their emotions and their actions, even when those thoughts are incorrect. When we don't challenge our perceptions, we behave as if what we are thinking is always true. A common goal of therapy is to help people recognize and challenge inaccurate thoughts and beliefs. I'll often ask people to record their thoughts at the end of the day, usually connecting them to some event or emotion. By charting the thoughts for a week or so, a person can start to notice certain patterns involving situations, emotions, and behaviors. Then we can start to challenge the internal dialogue and explore new ways of thinking.

Keep in mind that not every negative or untrue thought is directly from Satan; sometimes our notions come from our experiences of being a broken human with a limited viewpoint living amongst other broken humans. However, by paying attention to your inner commentary, you can step back and consider whether your thoughts are valid, helpful, or constructive. You can then challenge the ones that seem unhealthy, unhelpful, misguided, or downright destructive. Filling your mind with Scripture and aligning your thoughts with the truth are beautiful ways to start refuting the ideas that may be from the enemy or may not serve us well.

Here is an exercise to help you become more aware of your thoughts and thinking patterns (and extra bonus points if you can challenge them with Scripture like Jesus did!). Let me provide an example:

Situation

A friend doesn't text back when you ask how they are.

Thoughts

"I must have done something wrong."

"They must be upset with me."

"I always mess up my friendships."

"I am a horrible friend."

Emotion

Anxiety and worry

Behavior

Eat a gallon of ice cream and watch trash TV. That always stops this pain.

Talk negatively to others about the friend to others.

Alternative Thought

"Maybe my friend is busy or sick. I will give it some time and try to call before I get anxious."

"If my friend is upset with me, I will ask to talk about it and work out what went wrong."

God's Word

"Do not be anxious about anything, but in every situation, by prayer and petition, with thanksgiving, present your requests to God. And the peace of God, which transcends all understanding, will guard your hearts and your minds in Christ Jesus."

—Philippians 4:6–7

Whether that negative thought came from the enemy, from past experiences, or even from your sensitive personality, it can be challenged and replaced. As we get good at this, we strengthen our minds to resist our enemy's words when he does show up.

Here is another example. Sometimes, thoughts can build on each other as you find yourself on a destructive path:

Situation

It's the day after a fight with your husband.

Thought

"John doesn't appreciate me. He's not the man I married."

Emotion

Unloved, angry, and hurt

Behavior

Talk to Sam; he's always funny and compliments me and makes me feel better about myself.

Thought

"I deserve the attention Sam gives me—not the grief John gives me."

Emotion

Lonely and frustrated with John

Behavior

Flirting with Sam to get more positive attention and interaction

Alternative Thoughts

"John and I are experiencing conflict because we are married and closely connected. If I married anyone else there would be conflict there as well. I love John and I know he loves me too. Maybe we should do some things together to have more positive interactions or learn how to manage conflict by talking to a counselor. Our relationship is worth protecting and working on.

God's Word

"Be completely humble and gentle; be patient, bearing with one another in love."

—Ephesians 4:2

To challenge thoughts, you need to be able to step back and observe them. Since thoughts are so automatic, it may help to pay attention to when you have a shift in emotion. Notice when you become worried, anxious, sad, or angry. When you feel an emotion pop up, this should be an indication that something happened (situation) and your mind is responding to that situation (thought), which is impacting your emotions. When you feel the emotion or notice an emotion being expressed in your body, such as tightness, tension, or heaviness, try to name the emotion (this step can slow you down before you react) and find a way to record your thoughts. Some people carry a notebook or use a notes app on their phone. Record the situation, the emotion, and any thoughts you can remember having.

Next, see if you can challenge those thoughts. Can you broaden your perspective? Can you offer alternative explanations to the situation? Can you think of any Scripture verses that can help reframe the situation? As you spend time in the Word of God, the Lord will bring verses to mind when you need to challenge unhelpful or unhealthy thoughts. If you can't think of any, use the internet as a tool. For example, look up "verses about sadness" or "verses about worry" in your search engine to find verses to help you. Remember, using the Word of God is how Jesus showed us to resist the enemy. He promises to help us so that we, too, can resist our enemy with the Word of God. I also challenge you to commit God's Word to memory. Memorizing Scripture makes it's easily accessible when we need it. Bringing it to mind can be a powerful way to rebuke any negative thoughts.

> ***"We demolish arguments and every pretension that sets itself up against the knowledge of God, and we take captive every thought to make it obedient to Christ."* —2 Corinthians 10:5**

Keep in mind that not every negative or untrue idea comes from Satan, but he seems to primarily infiltrate our thoughts. The fruit from the tree of the knowledge of good and evil did not appeal to Eve until Satan worked on her thought process about it. The idea he planted—that God was withholding from her and did not speak truth—ultimately led her to make that detrimental choice to eat the fruit. We are taught to take our thoughts captive and test them for truth and goodness.

We may have a very sly enemy, but we also have a promise. For those who identify with Christ, God will crush Satan under our feet, which means that through the power of God given to us by the Holy Spirit, we have victory over Satan and his destructive tactics in our lives.

> ***"The God of peace will soon crush Satan under your feet. The grace of our Lord Jesus be with you."* —Romans 16:20**

Discussion Questions and Reflective Journaling Prompts

Can you think of a time when you have felt tempted to do something that would end up harming yourself or others?

Do you see that the enemy of your soul is seeking to tempt you in some way or lead you to distrust God?

Can you see the world's systems at war with God's Kingdom? In what ways do you see this playing out in the world today?

Do you see that the enemy of your soul is seeking to tempt you in some way or lead you to distrust God?

Talk or journal about a time when you experienced temptation.

Prayer

Lord, help me to pay attention to my thoughts. Give me discernment to recognize the difference between thoughts that help me and those that would lead me to harm. Give me the ability to challenge thoughts that may be from the enemy or may be based on my own faulty beliefs. Plant Your Word within my heart and mind so that I may be ready to defeat my enemy's influence on me just as Jesus did when He resisted the temptations of the enemy. Amen.

Chapter Four

The Fall's Impact on Humanity

The characters experience crisis-Part 1

Then the man and his wife heard the sound of the Lord God as he was walking in the garden in the cool of the day, and they hid from the Lord God among the trees of the garden. But the Lord God called to the man, "Where are. You?" He answered, "I. heard you in the garden, and I was afraid because I was naked, so. I hid." And he said "Who told you that you were naked? Have you eaten from the tree that I commanded you not to eat from?"
Genesis 3:8-11 NIV

Chapter 4 The Fall's Impact on Humanity

Truth be told, we don't need an enemy to live a life that is marked with pain or regret or seems futile and sometimes even self-destructive. After the fall, man became separated from God and distrustful of others. We have knowledge of good and evil with no real power to impact evil on our own. We have become vulnerable to disease and will eventually die. The work that we do, whether within the family or in the workforce, has become at times difficult and frustrating.

We have developed a plethora of unhealthy coping mechanisms to deal with this reality, but they wreck us. We do whatever we can to avoid pain and seek pleasure, even if the short-term benefits of our chosen coping method have long-term consequences. Consider that Adam and Eve's own son committed the first murder—of his brother. Cain, in an attempt to get rid of the source of his shame—and fearing the scarcity of God's blessing even though God assured him that if he did right, he, too, would be accepted (see Genesis 4:7)—acted out his jealous rage and killed Abel. It did not take long in the course of human history for us to display our brokenness.

Paul wrote about this internal struggle with our broken sin nature in the New Testament:

> ***"So, I find this law at work: Although I want to do good, evil is right there with me. For in my inner being I delight in God's law; but I see another law at work in me, waging war against the law of my mind and making me a prisoner of the law of sin at work within me. What a wretched man I am! Who will rescue me from this body that is subject to death? Thanks be to God, who delivers me through Jesus Christ our Lord!"***
> ***Romans 7:21–25.***

It is only in Jesus that we find our true hope.

In our fallen nature, we have at our core a focus on survival and pain avoidance. We can easily become addicted to activities and substances. We sometimes struggle with the concept of "enough" as we go to extremes needing more and more of what temporarily soothes the ache inside. This can push us to unhealthy extremes. For example, we can be workaholics or lazy. We can be people-pleasers or completely self-absorbed; we can be harshly judgmental of ourselves and others or we can be overly accepting of all things. We can be too clingy or too closed off. There is no end to the ways we can find to hurt ourselves and others, often those we love. When we lean on our own abilities, our own resources, and our own understanding, we will struggle to find lasting peace and joy. We may know that we are on the wrong path, but we struggle to find a way to change direction.

I want to mention some things that the mental health field doesn't often address. Therefore, our culture has a hard time understanding them—concepts like shame, guilt, and sin. These loaded words come with so much undeserved baggage that they lose their ability to guide and convict us in a healthy way. Many secular mental health providers are in the business of helping people to assuage the feelings of guilt and shame, and they certainly don't mention the forbidden word "sin." Mostly, that is because they don't use a spiritual lens to understand and to heal the pain of shame.

Honestly, many churches find it taboo to mention those concepts as well. Some have used those terms to wound and destroy others rather than pointing them to true healing. I've worked with many people who have gotten the wrong message from church about sin and shame. And those ideas need to be corrected. Religion sometimes exploits hurting people by telling them they are being punished for sin when they are actually suffering the effects of living in a broken world or suffering from the effects of the brokenness of others.

The Bible makes it clear that we can't always connect suffering with sin.

> ***"There is something else meaningless that occurs on earth: the righteous who get what the wicked deserve, and the wicked who get what the righteous deserve. This too, I say, is meaningless" Ecclesiastes 8:14***

Other times, people minimize or refuse to deal with their shame or brokenness. Remember, shame doesn't go away because we refuse to see it in ourselves, but we have many ways to avoid dealing with the pain of shame. A common defense mechanism is projection. This is seeing the things you don't like about yourself in other people. Projection is often combined with denial, which is the refusal to see your own flaws. Rationalization is another defense mechanism where people come up with excuses to deal with their wrong thoughts and behavior. I'm sure you can think of examples of these defense mechanisms. If you are honest, you may see examples in yourself. I have also found myself employing these defenses at one time or another to justify myself when I'm experiencing the pain associated with shame. We can twist the truth in so many ways to avoid taking responsibility for our actions and to avoid the pain that comes with shame. But none of these solutions truly remove our guilt or shame.

We need to see ourselves clearly. In doing so, we not only get in touch with our true condition but also get in touch with our true worth, identity, and the privilege we have to bring our brokenness to a loving God for forgiveness for what we've done and healing for what's been done against us. We are His kids. We are His treasure. He longs to remove our shame. Also, He wants the best for us and from us and loves us enough to correct and convict us when we, like Adam and Eve, are hiding in our sin and shame.

"Do not make light of the Lord's discipline, and do not lose heart when he rebukes you, because the Lord disciplines the one, he loves, and he chastens everyone he accepts as his son. Endure hardship as discipline; God is treating you as his children. For what children are not disciplined by their father? If you are not disciplined—and everyone undergoes discipline—then you are not legitimate, not true sons and daughters at all."
Hebrews 12:5–8

From the Therapist's Office

It is not unusual for people to want to talk about their dreams. I've heard about many dreams over the years and have noticed some common themes—not being prepared for a test, losing teeth, running in slow motion from a threat. Because I believe that dreams are the way the subconscious works out emotions, events, or concerns, I usually ask people to explore the emotional content and symbolic meaning of their dreams. I'll often ask what certain aspects of their dream mean to them.

Janet has a reoccurring dream of giving a presentation at work only to look down and notice that she has forgotten to get dressed. The emotions she experiences are humiliation and deep embarrassment.

Naked dreams are common and almost always combined with feelings of shame, humiliation, or vulnerability. I think they are so common because at our core, like Adam and Eve, we feel deep shame in being exposed—not just physical nakedness but spiritual nakedness. We don't want to come face to face with shame and our inability to truly hide from it. We've been struggling with vulnerability and shame ever since Adam and Eve were banished from Eden.

I have noticed as I've worked with people to explore the various problems they face that shame is often a common underlying theme. Therapy is about providing a safe, supportive, non-judgmental environment for people to open up and explore things about themselves. These issues are sometimes difficult to reveal to themselves, let alone anyone else, including a counselor. These vulnerable areas often cause feelings of deep embarrassment and perhaps guilt. And these feelings are often experienced as intense and intolerable pain. Sometimes this shame doesn't even fit with anything the person has done but instead stems from an act done to them, such as when someone has been abused.

At its core, shame signals there is something fundamentally wrong with you. And according to God's Word, this sense of "falling short" is true—in terms of our righteousness—not just about you, but about *all* of us. Because of the events we've discussed at the beginning of our existence, we all experience this human condition of sinfulness, and I have to believe that we would not experience shame if we didn't also know on a deep level that there is more to us than that. Shame reveals an ache to return fully to our forgotten memory of our former innocence and belonging with God. Shame signals an incongruency within us that we are not what we were meant to be. It is our heart's cry for help. We are God's beloved creation, beautifully and wonderfully made in His image to reflect His goodness. But sometimes, the shame gets in the way of us being able to experience that truth and live it out. We often spend our lives seeking ways to outrun the shame or keep it deeply hidden, while God is always seeking us, calling us to come out of hiding, ready to clothe us with the righteousness of Christ and remove our shame.

Please know that God deals compassionately with our shame. Our fear of judgment and punishment can keep us from turning toward our Savior. And either purposefully or inadvertently, the church sometimes sends the message that broken humans are not accepted. But the Bible tells us a different story.

> ***"For God did not send his Son into the world to condemn the world, but to save the world through him."***
> ***John 3:17***

He saves us when we come out of hiding and reach out to him for help. As we start to recognize our brokenness and recognize how it leads us to engage in that which damages our relationship to ourselves, others, or God, we can acknowledge the pain we bring to ourselves and others by way of confession to God. His desire is to separate us from our sin and shame. When we accept that Jesus died for us, that He took on our shame and, in exchange, clothed us in His righteousness once and for all, we are then made new. We are promised that our shame no longer defines us.

When we commit to surrendering our lives to Jesus and recognize the ineffective and sometimes harmful ways we try to manage our lives, we allow the Holy Spirit to transform us. Progressively, we become free from the power that shame has held in our lives. We start to experience ourselves as His beloved children. Please grasp what that means. The good God of the Universe who has made everything—who is gentle, compassionate, kind, and merciful—wants to gather you in His arms and love, lead, and protect you as His precious child. He wants to heal your brokenness.

We will still fail at times and make mistakes, but all children do that. If you have children, you know this to be true. But you don't lose your love, care, or concern for those children. You teach, train, and encourage them. God, whose love is far greater than our love as human parents, understands and cares for us so much more than the most loving and nurturing mother or father loves their child.

God's Answer to Guilt and Shame

When God looked down upon the world, He found no one righteous. So, He sent Jesus to be the righteousness for those who put their trust in Him. Remember—no one can be righteous on their own. We are all together in this condition. And this is where Satan will use one of two tactics. He may exploit our shame. He will tell us that we *are* alone in shame and far worse than others. He will whisper that we are different, unredeemable, and less than everyone else. These, my friends, are nothing but the lies of the deceiver. Beware of these deceits that make a person want to hide and isolate. They can cause someone to feel worthless. These deceptions blind a person from the truth that they are precious and made in the image of God. Conversely, we may also be tempted to look at others and feel far better than them. Consider Jesus's parable in the book of Luke.

> ***To some who were confident of their own righteousness and looked down on everyone else, Jesus told this parable: "Two men went up to the temple to pray, one a Pharisee and the other a tax collector. The Pharisee stood by himself and prayed: 'God, I thank you that I am not like other people—robbers, evildoers, adulterers—or even like this tax collector. I fast twice a week and give a tenth of all I get.'***
>
> ***"But the tax collector stood at a distance. He would not even look up to heaven, but beat his breast and said, 'God, have mercy on me, a sinner.'***
>
> ***"I tell you that this man, rather than the other, went home justified before God. For all those who exalt themselves will be humbled, and those who humble themselves will be exalted." Luke 18:9-14***

By comparing himself to a tax collector, the Pharisee feels justified, which allows him to avoid dealing with the shame of his own brokenness. If Satan can compel us to believe we aren't "that bad"—in other words, a "good person"—we may never deal appropriately with the brokenness in our life. We may never be able to see the part we play in our own challenging relationships and circumstances. And if we can't see our contribution to our problems, we can't effectively seek a solution.

Shame is meant to compel us to run into the arms of the One who longs to take it away. Shame is meant to nudge our hearts to call out to the One who covers us with His righteousness and calls us His beloved. God is the One who searches for us to rescue us from the pit of shame. Shame should not keep us hidden and isolated. Shame should not make us distort our own view of ourselves. This is our enemy's desire for us, not God's.

However, sometimes our own experiences with others have reinforced this distortion. Somewhere along the line, we learn that we can't be less than perfect, and this deceit becomes very difficult when a voice within us reminds us that we are *not* perfect. We will try throughout our lives to manage this incongruency in all kinds of unhealthy ways. If this applies to you, please seek godly counsel, someone with wisdom to help you see your worth and value in God's eyes just as you are. Your imperfection is part of being human, and God does not ask us to perfect ourselves. He understands we cannot do so. We become perfect only in our identification with Christ. He is the gift to us for the ultimate dilemma we find ourselves in, the inability to ever be perfect!

"For by one sacrifice, he has made perfect forever those who are being made holy." —Hebrews 10:14

Even when you know that your identity rests in being a beloved child of God, you can still experience guilt. Guilt, just like shame, has gotten a bad rap, especially in the mental health field I work in. However, hear me out. Guilt is about our behavior. It doesn't touch the core of our identity. Guilt can be viewed as the nagging feeling we have about things we shouldn't be doing, as God is transforming us more and more into who we were always meant to be. Guilt can motivate us to correct our behavior, to reconcile with others and with God, and to stay humbly aware of our tendency toward the brokenness of sin.

However, just as Satan exploits and twists our view of shame, he can also exploit or manipulate our feelings of guilt. Just like with shame, he can encourage us to minimize or justify our wrong behavior to avoid dealing with it. But he is also called our accuser. Where God convicts us in order to draw us to Him, Satan condemns us in an attempt to destroy our sense of worth and drive us from God. He is continually accusing us of failing. Remember, God does not hold those accusations against those who trust in Jesus, but Satan still can deceive us in our own thoughts.

I have worked with people who ruminate over incidents and conversations looking for where they may have messed up. Some people are so racked with chronic guilt as they strive for perfection that they cannot rest in the knowledge of being unconditionally loved by God as they are. In the counseling office, we may say these people have a loud inner critic.

If you've ever struggled with crippling guilt, I would advise you to become like a gentle parent to yourself or a good friend. Imagine speaking to yourself the way you would to someone you love who has made a mistake or to a child who stumbles and falls as they are learning to walk. You wouldn't chastise them. You would soothe them, encourage them, and speak kindly to them. If you still find this difficult, meditate on Scripture, which confirms how God sees you and speaks to you.

Tools of the Trade

These are some Scripture verses you can memorize and meditate on to remind yourself how God see you when you are struggling with a harsh inner critic.

- *"Therefore, there is now no condemnation for those who are in Christ Jesus."* —Romans 8:1
- *"Blessed is the one whose transgressions are forgiven, whose sins are covered. Blessed is the one whose sin the Lord does not count against them and in whose spirit is no deceit."* —Psalm 32:1–2
- *"My sacrifice, O God, is a broken spirit; a broken and contrite heart you, God, will not despise."* —Psalm 51:17
- *"As a father has compassion on his children, so the Lord has compassion on those who fear him; for he knows how we are formed, he remembers that we are dust."* —Psalm 103:13–14
- *"Therefore, as God's chosen people, holy and dearly loved, clothe yourselves with compassion, kindness, humility, gentleness and patience."* —Colossians 3:12

Here are some phrases you could try to speak as you work to tame any guilt or shame that is more condemning (destroying your worth) than convicting (confirming your worth).

- Mistakes are opportunities for learning and growth.
- Nobody is perfect and I don't have to be either.
- I am loved, even when I mess up or make mistakes.
- Every day is a new beginning.
- If God's mercies are new every morning, I, too, will give myself grace.
- Progress, not perfection.

- I can trust that God helps me in my weakness.
- My journey is not complete; I am still learning and growing.

Giving yourself grace and compassion is an important way to see yourself through God's eyes. Dear friend, I pray you let God's love for you become the way you experience yourself. God's grace is sufficient for your brokenness. What a relief to let that sink in and experience a God who doesn't wait for you to be perfect before lavishing you with love.

By the way, it is not wrong to have self-love. When we see ourselves as worthy of grace and compassion and love, we are in the position to see and treat others that way as well. Self-love, which I'll define as a belief in being worthy of love or lovable, can open our hearts to the overflowing of God's love. This love is absolutely transformational. Imagine a great thirst to be loved by your heavenly Father. He not only fills the empty cup you hold out but provides a source that never runs out, one that overflows your own cup and continues to flow so that it can be shared freely with others. This image of a cup overflowing is how I conceptualize the power of the abundant love of God by borrowing from the language of David in Psalm 23:5. My friends, I hope you can envision and experience this as well!

Discussion Questions and Reflective Journaling Prompts

How did Adam and Eve clothing themselves in fig leaves reflect how we try to deal with our shame?

God covered Adam and Eve with animal skins. How did this foreshadow the work He does to redeem us?

Why do you suppose that God put a flaming sword between Adam and Eve and the tree of life?

Do you have a strong inner critic? Do you think it helps you or keeps you in a struggle with guilt or shame?

Do you sense the difference between guilt and shame in your own life?

Prayer

Lord, I confess the ways I hide from you, from others, and even from myself. Reveal to me the things that need to change as I grow and change to be more like You. Help me to know that You do not expect perfection from me but that You seek me even as I hide from you, just as Adam and Eve hid from You. You long to bring me out of hiding and cover my shame so that I can enjoy a relationship with You and experience Your love. Give me the courage to truly be real with you. Amen.

Chapter Five

The Fall's Impact on Relationships

The characters experience crisis-Part 2

The man said, "This woman you put here with me-she gave me some fruit from the tree, and I ate it".
Genesis 3:10-12 NIV

Chapter 5 The Fall's Impact on Relationships

Because the fall impacted the entire human race, relationships, too, became broken from their perfected state. Where the individual was marked by shame, relationships became tarnished by blame. The posturing and posing and jockeying for positions began. There was finger-pointing and blame-shifting from the very start. Adam and Eve's relationship with God was marred, and so was Adam's relationship with Eve. Adam blamed Eve, while Eve blamed the serpent. And the serpent hissed "Ssssucccsessss." No one took responsibility for their choices. And the consequence was that relational brokenness has been passed down through the generations.

Humanity has become contaminated with blame, hatred, discord, grudges, envy, jealousy, mistrust, abuse, and betrayal. These are just some issues that can damage our most important relationships, and it's the reason so many of Jesus's teachings were about loving one another, forgiving one another, and bearing with one another. Ever since Genesis 3, loving other people, (especially our enemies) and forgiving them has often required great effort, yet this is how God calls His people to live together. We are more prone to hide our true selves from one another and from God, to blame each other, and to look out for ourselves first. That is why we are so inspired when we see someone acting with humility or sacrificially. We are aching for that in our relationships.

Some of the most intense sources of pain I've witnessed have resulted from severed relationships and/or betrayal. When God made Eve, He did so because it was not good for Adam to be alone. He created Adam to be relational as He is relational. As God was creating everything, He didn't refer to Himself as "I." He talked about Himself in the plural: "Let *us* make man in Our image" (Genesis 1:26–27). He created both male and female to reflect His goodness and glory. And He created them to help one another and experience intimacy with together. He created them to be securely attached to one another.

From the Therapist's Office

Janice and Roy sit separated from each other, both with arms crossed protectively across their bodies. Janice says she is exhausted and depressed. She tells me that she does all the household chores, manages the kids' homework and activities, and takes care of everything on weekends while her husband spends his weekends golfing and hunting with friends.

When I ask Roy to explain how he sees things, Roy reports that Janice doesn't really seem to want his help. He says she complains that he doesn't do anything right. He claims she scolds him and scowls at him when he attempts to pitch in, and this sends him the message to back off and go away. Janice disagrees; she believes he does a poor job helping to get out of doing any work so that he can go have fun. Roy believes Janice is never happy because she really doesn't want him to interfere with the very precise way she does things, so he disappears to do his own thing.

When we dive in deeper than the content of their argument and get to the emotional issues that drive the dance, they repeatedly find themselves in, we find that Janice feels deeply hurt when Roy leaves her to do all the work at home. The feeling she describes is being abandoned by the person she so desperately wants to feel supported by—she is left to shoulder the load that she finds overwhelming. In her attempts to express this deep hurt while trying to protect herself from vulnerability, she harshly criticizes Roy for being selfish and rushing through things so that he can leave her.

Janice's disparaging words strike at Roy's sense of shame and inadequacy. He fears not being enough for Janice, and as she calls him out on not being enough, his shame causes him to want to run away and hide from her. He does this by making plans with friends for the weekends. When he is away from Janice, he feels safe from the wounding, sharp jabs of her words. Both blame the other for the situation they find themselves in. Neither is willing to consider that the other might be experiencing pain that fuels their behavior. Both feel too afraid to risk vulnerability by expressing the pain they feel, so they behave in ways that keep the cycle going.

I see the impact of relational problems every day in my practice. It seems to be the main reason people come to therapy. I've seen parents grieving broken relationships with their adult children. I've seen adult children grappling with the pain of abuse, neglect, or childhood trauma at the hands of their parents. I've witnessed husband and wives confused, frustrated, hurt, or betrayed by marital issues. I've helped people dealing with the pain of broken friendships and people navigating the stress of difficult coworkers or bosses. Relationship issues are so messy and can be so painful, and we all experience them.

We struggle with the delicate balance of caring about another person while taking care of our own needs or asking for our own needs to be met. Many of our relational issues are not about right or wrong but about navigating competing needs and values. We tend to either shut down our needs or become demanding and say or do whatever we can to let someone else know they have mistreated us. We become passive or aggressive or passive-aggressive. It is so hard to be assertive, that healthy place in the middle. It can sometimes take a lot of strength to open up about how we want to be treated and be vulnerable enough to ask for what we need while also respecting another's choices, even if that choice is "no" to our request. It is hard to love or feel the emotion of love when we don't feel safe. It's sometime easier to blame someone else for the unhappy situations we find ourselves in. In this respect, we are not so unlike Adam and Eve.

Entire books have been written about how to develop healthy interpersonal skills to build sound relationships. In this limited space, I can't address all the ways relationships have suffered under the impact of the fall. Relationship difficulties are a result of two or more broken individuals trying to get a relationship right, which can create a multitude of combinations for how it can all go wrong. However, when you are struggling in a difficult relationship, the fall's effects can always be found at the core. When Adam and Eve disobeyed God and ate of the tree they were not to eat from, shame (and its counterpart, pride), scarcity, vulnerability, and fear entered the picture and have been passed along to all the generations that came after them. These issues negatively impact relationships.

If I could address just one thing I've noticed, its that good relationships are enjoyed by those who have developed the ability to successfully navigate competing needs through a variety of skills. These include experiencing and showing compassion, active listening, assertiveness, setting up healthy boundaries, engaging in good communication, and resolving conflict well. While those are all important skills, let's briefly go over some you can start practicing right now.

Tools of the Trade

Communication skills

One of the easiest skills to learn and hardest to implement if you haven't had much practice, is assertiveness. It is challenging because it requires vulnerability. Remember, after the fall, vulnerability doesn't feel so good. It can feel like a lack of safety and protection. It requires being open enough to recognize and validate your own needs and make healthy requests, while simultaneously respecting and validating another's need and their decision. Assertiveness involves being kind, respectful, straightforward, and firm without revenge or punishment. When we are assertive, we have good boundaries. We recognize that we can't force anyone to do our will, but we still need to make our requests known. It's important to respect another person's free will and thus respect their boundaries and choices. We make our desires known first by expressing how we feel, and second, by making the request.

Here is an example:

> "I feel frustrated when you show up late for dinner. I wish you would be on time next time or call ahead to let me know you are going to be late."

If someone doesn't honor your requests, don't punish them. Simply act within your sphere of control by exploring the options within your own boundaries. For example, you could choose to make a meal that will keep warm while waiting or choose to eat dinner alone and then sit with the other person later while they eat. More importantly, you can ask the other person to participate in finding a solution. This could be accomplished by saying something like,

> "Having dinner together is important to me. Can you think of a way we could make that work?"

This is so much better than the blame and shame game that often gets played in relationships. And sending blame or shame messages is usually not the best way to get your needs met. It often ends in defensiveness or counterattacks that can extend conflict and create relational distance.

Another skill that goes along with assertiveness is active or reflective listening. This is simply repeating back with as much understanding as possible what someone is saying.

Example:

> "You are frustrated that I am late, and you'd like me to work on being on time for dinner or letting you know when I'll be late."

When you get good at this, you can add more reflection into the statement:

> "You value eating dinner with me, and it frustrates you when I am running late. You'd like me to make dinner a priority to show you I appreciate spending time with you, too; is that correct?"

This demonstrates the ability to step away from your own perspective to let someone know you hear what they say. This validates their perspective even if you don't agree with them, and you send the message, "I hear you. I'm tracking with what you are saying."

Active listening lets us know when we aren't tracking. It happens more than we realize. We think we hear what another is saying, but it's been filtered through the lens of our past experiences and personal expectations, and we often get it wrong. Reflecting back what someone says gives them a chance to correct us so that we can track their communication better.

Practicing assertiveness can be difficult for those who fear rejection and abandonment. These core fears are perhaps potential within all of us as remnants of the fall, but generally they are activated in childhood when an individual's needs are not adequately met by primary caregivers. When a person is afraid that others will reject or dismiss their needs, they fear the vulnerability of exposing those needs and may say nothing about their emotions or wishes. (This can lead to passivity—it can often create resentment within the person who can't articulate their needs but is disappointed and frustrated nonetheless when their needs aren't noticed or met.) Alternatively, to avoid their own vulnerability, a person may become aggressive, making demands and offering criticism. An example of this would be, "You're such a jerk—you don't even care that I've been preparing you a hot dinner. You only care about yourself. Make sure you're home on time tomorrow or you can make your own dinner!"

While aggressiveness can protect the self from the vulnerability and pain of making a request that could be denied, it also creates more conflict and less connection in a relationship.

Repairing skills

Inevitably, we will mess up. We will wound or be wounded in our relationships. That's what happens when broken people are in relationships together. Knowing how to repair well after conflict is so important. Repairing requires the skills of asking for forgiveness and granting forgiveness.

Asking for forgiveness requires self-awareness, humility, and vulnerability. It is the ability to know when your own personal struggles to win, survive, strike back, or seek pleasure harm the other person and harm the relationship. It requires the ability to admit our wrongdoings, apologize, and ask to be forgiven. Asking for forgiveness is a forgotten art, even among Christians. It is biblical and, in my opinion, should be re-established in our relationships as it promotes humility and intimacy.

An offense may be something that can be quickly repaired, or it may take a third party through counseling to walk through the pain. Granting forgiveness can be equally as tough, depending on the offense. It requires feeling the pain of the rupture and releasing the offense for the healing of the relationship. Holding onto an offense can give us the feeling of justification and power over the other person. This is not to discount the injustice, but forgiveness is an act of covering that injustice with grace.

Depending on the situation, granting forgiveness may require the vulnerability to once again trust the person who caused pain. Releasing the offense may feel like releasing some protective power over the pain someone caused us. But it usually results in releasing the power of bitterness, preventing it from taking root in the offended one's heart. Repairing a relationship wound can be challenging, but many of those who walk through the process with the skills of asking for and granting forgiveness both in word and in deed often describe experiencing a relationship that is deeper and richer because of the power of those skills. It may require help from a skilled professional, and it most certainly requires the help of the Holy Spirit. The Spirit empowers us to lay down our grievances and our demands for justice as we represent to others the very thing that God does for us. By asking for and granting forgiveness, we are living out the redemptive power that limits the fall's effects on relationships.

Sometimes, forgiveness is granted but the relationship cannot experience healing because nothing has changed. You have probably heard it said, "If nothing changes, nothing changes." And that goes for relationships as well as everything else. When we forgive, we often still need to set boundaries. When we do this, we are holding people accountable for their behavior, which in some cases is necessary to help them stop destructive behavior to the degree that it is within our ability to do so. We cannot change another person, but we can establish our own boundaries to limit the damage their behavior can do to us.

Remember that God put Adam and Eve together to meet one another's needs for companionship, security, and safety, not only for themselves but also for their children. This gives us a picture of God's intention for human relationships. Marriages, friendships, and family relationships flourish when each person recognizes the value of their needs *and* the other person's, and they make it a priority to apologize and grant forgiveness for failures. When we give others respect and have a mutual expectation of also being respected and cared for, we can risk becoming vulnerable without fear of being hurt for exposing our most important and intimate needs. Vulnerability is scary, but in the context of a healthy relationship, it is the only way to experience true intimacy.

In a relationship where two people can truly feel safe with one another, healing can occur within that deep wound we all have to some extent, the one stemming from that ancient first experience with shame that causes us to hide from one another. So many good resources are available for building healthy relationships. And there is almost no greater investment in your personal healing and future legacy than in making healthy relationships a priority. Sometimes we need to recognize and break bad relational patterns passed down through previous generations. The time we spend focusing on developing, maintaining, and healing relationships will be a worthy pursuit in challenging the effects of the fall in our lives and in the lives of those who come after us.

I want to address those without a partner or with a challenging partner, who may find the above topic irrelevant, perhaps even painful. This is just a reminder that our most supreme and secure relational attachment is with God Himself. Throughout the Bible, God is sending the message that He will not abandon those who belong to Him. He develops and creates the covenant between Himself and Israel in the Old Testament. And in the New Testament, as the power of Christ's work extends to the world, we are all given the opportunity to become His beloved children, each of whom is known and loved deeply and individually. Please memorize these verses—post them where you can always see them and rest in the secure attachment to a God who loves you and will never leave you.

- *"And surely, I am with you always, to the very end of the age."* —Matthew 28–20
- *"For I am convinced that neither death nor life, neither angels nor demons, neither the present nor the future, nor any powers, neither height nor depth, nor anything else in all creation, will be able to separate us from the love of God that is in Christ Jesus our Lord."* —Romans 8:38–39
- *"The Lord is close to the brokenhearted and saves those who are crushed in spirit."* —Psalm 34:18
- *The Lord himself goes before you and will be with you; he will never leave you nor forsake you. Do not be afraid; do not be discouraged."* —Deuteronomy 31:8

Discussion Questions and Reflective Journaling Prompts

How have you experienced the effects of the fall on your relationships? Write or talk about your experiences.

What evidence do you have that relationships are important to God?

Have you experienced being forgiven or asking for forgiveness? What was that like for you?

Prayer

Dear Lord, You have made me relational because my relationships can be such a source of healing and help to me and to others. My relationships, when at their best, can reflect Your relational character and can make me strong against the challenges of life. Help me to love others well, to resolve conflicts quickly, and to treat others with lovingkindness. Help me to overcome my own relationship wounds and leave a loving legacy for those who come after me. Remind me that You are relational in nature, and in relationship with You, I am always securely attached to Your love no matter my circumstance. Amen.

Chapter Six

How the Fall Impacted the entire creation

The setting experiences crisis

For the creation was subjected to frustration, not by its own choice, but by the will of the one who subjected it, in hopes that the creation itself will be liberated from its bondage to decay and brought into the freedom and glory of the children of God. We know that the whole creation has been groaning as in the pains of childbirth right up to the present time.
Romans 8:20-22 NIV

Chapter 6 How the Fall Impacted the Entire Creation

Recently, the world collectively experienced the challenges of living in a pandemic. The problems brought to therapy sessions were wide-ranging and universal. People struggled with so much loss—loss of community, loss of gathering together, loss of freedoms. Some people lost their job or businesses, while others lost their health or their loved ones. Kids lost out on socializing and educational opportunities provided by in-person school and all the extra-curricular activities associated with it. Older kids lost their graduation ceremonies and proms, along with other normal high school and college experiences.

The building blocks of security, connection, routine, and structure were shaken. Along with loss, people suffered many different fears: fear of exposure to the virus, fear of death, fear of vaccination, fear of having to go to the hospital, and fear of isolation. People feared each other and different points of view. Families were often divided.

People experienced a variety of stressors—the stress of not being able to obtain goods and not being able to travel (especially to see loved ones). People endured the stress of balancing work and school all within the confines of home. For the frontline health care workers, the stress level was particularly intense. They faced daily exposure to the virus while dealing with the fears and isolation of those who were sick. They were thrown into new procedures and sometimes situations that were understaffed and chaotic. Those of us working in the mental health field were trying to help very anxious and depressed clients navigate these issues—often over telehealth platforms that were unfamiliar for many of us and sometimes glitchy.

The recent pandemic is an example of how living in a broken world—a world with disease and discord—will impact our physical, mental, and emotional health. When we add in other broken areas such as poverty, injustice, corrupt social or government systems, and the devastation brought on by war or natural disasters, we can truly feel as if the whole world is groaning and begging for relief.

The earth has indeed been cursed, as we read in Genesis, and we still feel the effects today:

To the woman he said, "I will make your pains in childbearing very severe; with painful labor you will give birth to children. Your desire will be for your husband, and he will rule over you." To Adam he said, "Because you listened to your wife and ate fruit from the tree about which I commanded you, 'You must not eat from it,' Cursed is the ground because of you; through painful toil you will eat food from it all the days of your life. It will produce thorns and thistles for you, and you will eat the plants of the field. By the sweat of your brow, you will eat your food until you return to the ground, since from it you were taken; for dust you are and to dust you will return."
Genesis 3:16–19

After he was cast out of Eden, Adam learned that delicious food wasn't freely available from the trees. Initially, Adam had to struggle with the earth, contending with the elements, pests, weeds, and rocks to grow food and survive. Eve would experience difficulties in relationship. Her husband would have authority over her, and her children would bring her pain.

We continue to experience the effects of living in a world that has been impacted by the brokenness of all of creation. Through the curse on Adam and Eve, God indicated that there would be troubles in the arenas of work and family, men and women's traditional spheres of influence. But as joint image bearers of God, we have a tremendous opportunity to continually bring order out of the chaos, to use the creativity God has given us to come up with innovative solutions, and to experience our work as productive and meaningful even in its difficulty. Considering how far the human race has come since Adam, how much we've been able to create and learn to do, we can see that there is still order, creativity, and innovation within the chaos of the world systems. We can see that our work, no matter what we have been assigned to do, should be about bringing peace and restoring order, again and again sometimes, while caring for and nurturing children, pets, or plants. We should be removing obstacles, healing, building, repairing, or innovating.

When we do these things in the midst of our broken world, our lives reflect the One who is making all things new. Through the work He gives us, no matter if it's fixing teeth, fixing toilets, or fixing broken toys, whether it's healing hearts physically or emotionally or finding innovative solutions to tough problems, we are as mirrors reflecting the One True Light back to the world. This light can be a source of hope to others even in the darkness of this cursed world. We are charged to partner with God as co-stewards of the earth and participate with Him in creating goodness here. As it says in Matthew 6:10, "Your kingdom come, your will be done on earth as it is in heaven." As followers of Jesus, it's our prayer, our vision, and our commission to obediently bring everything under the will of God as much as it is in our power to do so in our little corner of the world.

From the Therapist's Office

Leslie is being simultaneously bombarded with a list of stressors that have all impacted her within the last several months. Her parents' home was recently in the path of out-of-control wildfires, forcing them to evacuate for a while and live with Leslie and her family. Leslie then experienced flooding in her own home, resulting in time-consuming and expensive cleanup afterword. Her husband has recently had some skin cancer removed, and her daughter is getting tested for food allergies that might be contributing to her various health problems. Leslie laments, "I feel as if the entire planet is against us." Indeed, it feels like we work hard for our home and our health and our family's well-being, and sometimes it seems like uncontrollable forces threaten to undo all our efforts.

As Genesis 3:16–19 forewarned, we can certainly see and experience that life's work is filled with stress. Nothing important or meaningful that we do is going to be without some stress. Even if we love what we do, it will not always easy or completely fulfilling. We will from time to time run into roadblocks, frustrations, or even outright disasters. Resilient people have found ways to bend and not break under pressure and to bounce back from the stressors of life—whether they arise from pressures at work, challenging family issues, or world problems, such as a pandemic or political unrest.

Tools of the Trade

There are some ways to increase resiliency to reduce the negative impact of stress. Below are a few things you can do to better cope with the stressors you will inevitably experience in life.

Sleep
Getting plenty of sleep is so important. Sleep is the essential foundation to stress resilience. I recommend that my clients make it a priority to get the required seven to eight hours per night. That might involve making your environment better conducive to sleep. For example, do not consume caffeine in the afternoon or evening. Stop exposure to blue light screens two hours before bed. Keep your room temperature cool. Having a relaxing bedtime routine that sets the stage for sleep and relaxes the body are all simple things you can do to promote sleep.

Exercise
Physical activity is also important for stress reduction. Getting thirty minutes a day of some form of exercise is recommended. Exercise is a way to release the pent-up energy of stress, to produce endorphins that help you feel good, and to keep your body in good health to better handle stress.

Relaxation rituals
Mindfulness meditation, prayer time, and stretching-based exercise routines (such as yoga), as well as the mindful walk introduced before, have been shown to reduce the negative impact of stress. These relaxation skills activate the parasympathetic nervous system responsible for rest and repair of our bodies and mind.

Rest
God has given us the sabbath, a day to rest from our work. It is meant to rejuvenate and replenish us. Many of us have forgotten to observe and fully embrace a day of rest once a week. But setting aside this weekly time to stop our normal routines and recenter your life on worship and rejuvenation can do wonders to help you manage stress. Enjoying rest-filled vacations occasionally during the year and taking moments in the day to stop and inhale some slow, deep breaths are all ways to build more rest into your life.

Play (rest's fun cousin!)
If it is hard to find joy in your work, please make it a priority to play. I believe that when we play, we experience the creative, curious, joyful nature of God. Whether your play is active and adventure-seeking or relaxing and restful, you

can find joy and fulfillment when you play. If the thought of play doesn't resonate with you, I encourage you to think about what you enjoyed doing most as a kid. When did you lose yourself in something? I was a nature nerd. Yep, I organized my very own Nature Club and gathered my friends at a pond on a vacant lot in our neighborhood to gather pond samples to study under the microscope. Today, I find the greatest enjoyment outdoors in nature, whether that is gardening, walking the beach, feeding birds, or growing butterflies (as I talked about earlier)—this is where my soul finds rest and joy. When I am outside immersed in nature, the stress I feel from the challenges of the world melts away for a time.

Your childhood fun may have been in organized sports, making things, playing music, or collecting things. Whatever you enjoyed as a child was probably something you were innately drawn to. Play can be enjoyed for life. What were you playing as a child that you may have let go of or forgotten—and how can you find a way now to incorporate a similar kind of play into your life?

Meaning making

Finding meaning in the work we do helps us stay resilient to the stress associated with our work. Think about the ways you are challenged by living in a broken world. Now try to see the significance of your work despite the challenges. Can you see that even if you are doing repetitive tasks, you are bringing order out of chaos, rest for the weary, beauty out of ashes, or healing to the broken? Keep in mind, you are reflecting the image of God through your work. Our God brings the sun up daily; He brings the seasons around over and over to do the work of growth, harvest, and rest. He is a God who creates rhythms and routines and can be counted on to not grow weary of His repetitive and regenerative work.

> ***"As long as the earth endures, seedtime and harvest, cold and heat, summer and winter, day and night will never cease."***
>
> ***—Genesis 8:22***

Sometimes we find our work involves managing our own personal crisis and, in this sense, involves finding a way to understand and start to remove obstacles in our path, bringing forth growth or find meaning within grief and loss. As we do this work successfully, we can experience wisdom and healing.

Those who experience the power of healing can then become a source of healing and support to others. This, too, is redemptive work that reflects the Creator. He is the God who redeems our stories, and some of us can participate in making the world a better place based on the growth we experience from our own painful experiences. That is not an easy task, and it usually comes after much healing, but it can be an impactful result of a painful chapter in our story. It is a way of partnering with God in the work He is doing—restoring that which seems without hope.

The work you do in this world may be a result of the curse given to broken humans living in a broken world. It may seem futile or mundane. But God has given it to you as a gift, to work alongside Him to create, bring order, mend, heal, and reflect to the world a picture of His very nature.

> ***"See, I am doing a new thing! Now it springs up; do you not perceive it? I am making a way in the wilderness and streams in the wasteland."***
>
> ***—Isaiah 49:13***

> ***"He who was seated on the throne said, 'I am making everything new!' Then he said, 'Write this down, for these words are trustworthy and true.'"***
>
> **—Revelation 21:5**

When we do the assignments, He has entrusted to us, we are like lights shining in a dark world that desperately needs us.

Still not convinced that the work you do to try to bring order into your day or into the world is of any value? Maybe you are struggling with cleaning up messes that never should have happened, messes created by natural or human forces. Maybe the work of redemption is not within the clean-up and repair but within you. The suffering we experience living in a broken world can be used to grow us spiritually. Consider what God's Word says about our suffering-

> ***"We also glory in our sufferings, because we know that suffering produces perseverance; perseverance, character; and character, hope. And hope does not put us to shame, because God's love has been poured out into our hearts through the Holy Spirit, who has been given to us"***
>
> ***—Romans 5:3–6***

Discussion Questions and Reflective Journaling Prompts

In what way are you participating with God to reflect His goodness and bring His kingdom into a broken world?

Notice the correlation between creation groaning up until this present time as if in childbirth (Romans 8:20–22) and the curse on women who give birth to children in painful labor. Do you suppose there is a connection here? If so, what do you think God is revealing to us?

Do you think there is value in suffering? Have you ever experienced that?

Prayer

Dear Lord, I see evidence of so much brokenness in the world. I pray that "your kingdom come and your will be done on earth as it is in heaven." Let me be a kingdom builder for You in the sphere of work You have given me. Lord, let me delight in the tasks of creating order, keeping things running smoothly, encouraging and equipping others, and providing support for my family and loved ones. Give me periods of rest and relaxation to refuel me for the tasks at hand. Let me see that You have given me this work not to punish me but to grow and strengthen me spiritually and to allow me to participate with You in taking care of this broken world. Amen.

Chapter Seven

The Nature of God has Never Changed

How the Hero of our Story rescues us

For the Lord is good and his love endures forever: His faithfulness continues through all generations.
Psalm 100-5 NIV

"I am the Alpha and the Omega, the First and the Last, the Beginning and the End. Blessed are those who wash their robes, that they may have the right to the tree of life and may go through the gates into the city."
Revelation 22:13-14 NIV

Chapter 7 The Nature of God has Never Changed

God is and always has been good, gracious, patient, merciful, available, near to us, and involved in the redemption of His creation. The Old Testament shows God's redemptive work and points to Jesus as the hope for humanity. The New Testament records the story of His life, ministry, death, and resurrection and tells how the church sprung up to tell the good news of this intervening hope for the world.

The book of Revelation ends by describing the restoration of a new creation and a new city that has the elements of Eden itself. A garden later becomes a city for all who know and love God to dwell with Him forever. This is depicted as a place where there are no more tears or sadness, where there is abundance of light and life and everlasting communion with God. This is the hope of all who put their trust in Jesus, the One who saves us from the long-term repercussions of the fall and redeems our stories and sorrows and gives them purpose. You will see that the tree of life is there as well, but it is now available to those whose hope is in Jesus. Those who have been cleansed and made perfect through the redemptive work of Christ can take, eat, and live forever, no longer separated from God.

As we study the Word of God, we can begin to see that Jesus, Himself is the Living Word. He is woven throughout the Bible from beginning to end. Even right after the fall, when God clothed Adam and Eve in animal skins, He covered them with sacrificial grace. Their attempts to use garments of fig leaves wouldn't do—it had to be through sacrifice that their shame was covered. God didn't destroy them and make a new set of humans. He covered them, cleansed them, and saved them—all while immediately foreshadowing His perfect plan to rescue His creation. As God's word says, all "who were baptized into Christ have clothed yourselves with Christ." Galatians 3:27

> ***"I delight greatly in the Lord: my soul rejoices in my God. For he has clothed me with garments of salvation and arrayed me in a robe of his righteousness, as a bridegroom adorns his head like a priest, and as a bride adorns herself with her jewels."***
>
> ***—Isaiah 61:10***

When we understand and accept that Jesus alone can cover our shame and truly heal our brokenness, we become united with the only One who can break the curse that Adam left within us all. The image of a bride and bridegroom are a picture of a future reunification and perfect intimacy with God.

Paul assures us of this when He compares what we inherit from Adam to what we inherit in Jesus:

> ***"Consequently, just as one trespass resulted in condemnation for all people, so also one righteous act resulted in justification and life for all people. For just as through the disobedience of the one man the many were made sinners, so also through the obedience of the one man the many will be made righteous."***
>
> ***—Romans 5:18-19***

God's plan to reconcile us to Himself was initiated right there in the garden. It's told throughout all of history, which is His Story (and we are each included in this epic adventure and given a role to play). As His plan unfolds, it all points to Jesus and His redeeming work. He desires to renew us as individuals, heal our broken relationships, renew a broken world, and destroy our enemy. He invites us to participate with Him in bringing this glorious kingdom to Earth. Even as our enemy rages against Him and against us, we can trust that Satan's sting has been removed. Nothing can separate us from the God who loves us. We are assured that the same God who clothed Adam and Eve and gave them assignments will fulfill His plan to bring everything under His authority. He rules with justice and mercy and desires that no one shall perish.

But what do we do about the suffering we currently face as we exist somewhere in the middle of this grand story?

From the Therapist's Office

Brian and Elise have been given devastating news that their newborn baby has a genetic disorder and will most likely not live past the age of five . .

Katrina has just experienced the devasting blow that her sweet teenage daughter has taken her own life . . .

Melody's young husband has just been diagnosed with cancer.

When people come to therapy at the beginning of an intense life crisis like the examples above, it is sometimes challenging to know what to say or to find a way to truly help. This is often because I can't imagine the specific pain that they experience. However, I do know what it is to experience pain, to experience brokenness and grief. My experiences may not be the same as someone else's, but in our humanity we all experience the pain of grief, loss, fear, and heartbreak. We all at times experience the pain of our own brokenness.

So, in these situations, I know what not to say.

I will not say, "This is somehow God's plan."

I will not say, "Maybe God sees how strong your faith is and thinks you could handle it."

I will not even hint that this could be a result of them not having enough faith.

Words like those have wounded those who have heard them. Instead, I will sit with them in their shock and grief. I will pray with them if they would like. I will listen and bear witness, but I know not to give trite answers. In moments like these, people question, Is God good? Does He care? Has He abandoned me? So, I will be present. In time, I will help them express and process the emotions associated with grief, help them connect with supportive others who have walked a similar path, help them find practical resources, and continue to be available, providing a place where they can safely express whatever they need to express. I will pray that in some way God is showing up through me and through others who are also standing with them in this very difficult time, offering the hope that they are not alone, that they have not been abandoned.

It is the most difficult part of my job. I often feel inadequate in the face of such intense grief. But I know that those who are in pain need others to surround them in love. It is sometimes the only way we can truly help. In doing so, we are representing the God who does not leave us.

Take a moment to consider the pain or hardship that may have drawn you to this Bible study. I wish there were answers to the suffering that you experience or that you know exists in this world, but we are not always given answers. We are told quite clearly in the Bible that in this world we will have trouble (John 16:33). Pain and suffering seem to be the guarantee for us all at some point as we take our place and play our part in this story.

But along with this hard truth, we are also given the opportunity to be children of God, with the promise to one day live in His presence, where He will wipe every tear from our eyes. We will dwell with God and no longer feel a separation from Him. Everything will be set right; everything will be made new. One day, we will reach the final chapter of an incredible story, one fraught with crisis, pain, and tension. In this conclusion, we will find that the Hero was always with us and had a plan all along. Maybe from that future place looking back, even to where you are currently living, you will see that He has always been there with you. Things may one day make sense that today make no sense at all. That is my hope.

Sometimes when I read a book that seems like it is taking a very scary or dangerous turn, I will flip ahead to the end to see if the characters are okay. I know this takes the thrill out of the story unfolding before me. But sometimes I just have to find out. If I see that the characters are okay at the end, I can breathe a sigh of relief and go back to enjoying the story. Friends, we too have that ability—for what has happened and what will happen are written down in the Word of God. We, who know Him and put our trust in Him, will be okay. We will be more than okay.

Try to imagine what this future with God might be like—when we live with Him in a secure place, free from pain, fear, and death, with no more worldly disasters or painful relationships. Is it reminiscent of our imaginings of Eden? After thinking about it, know that it will be so much better than you ever could imagine. As you hold to this promise, have hope that one day the heavy clouds covering your current situation will part to reveal that the sun has always been there. It has never left—you just couldn't see it at times. Trust that life will not always be as it is right now. One day, you may see your circumstances from a different perspective. I hope you will hold on to that hope in your current situation. Remember this word from the apostle Paul: "I consider that our present sufferings are not worth comparing with the glory that will be revealed in us" (Romans 8:18).

Tools of the Trade

One of the most important concepts to grasp when coping with difficult situations is acceptance. Acceptance is not giving up, nor is it saying, "I'm okay with this." Acceptance is recognizing that there is a time to grieve and a time to accept—when you stop pouring energy into a situation that can't be changed so that you can direct your energy to that which can be changed.

In the stages of grief, acceptance is the final stage, so it comes after experiencing and processing many difficult emotions. But when acceptance occurs, energy can be used for "meaning making." This skill requires that you have taken time to process and heal from something difficult in your life. Acceptance doesn't mean that pain goes away, it just means coming to a place where you accept the ache without trying to change it, wish it away, or find ways to nurture it or numb it. It means turning everything over to God in an act of trust in His plan. It means finding a way to live with the ache without letting it take center stage in your life, consuming you or destroying you. It is an advanced skill and may be too difficult when wounds are fresh. In some cases, using this skill may take a very, very, long time. But when you can take what once seemed ruined or without hope and give it meaning and purpose, you become victorious over it.

Think back to a time when things didn't work out as you had hoped and planned—when pain made its home within you. Can you find a way to see how that situation helped you become the person you are today? Did it give you strength? Tenacity? Courage? Perhaps you became more compassionate of others, or maybe you became more dependent on God and closer to Him? Perhaps it gave you a mission or ministry to recognize a felt need to help others as you were helped, or it has enabled you to care for others in a way you wish you had been helped but weren't.

Many ministries and nonprofits have been born out of someone's pain in an attempt to provide a solution to a problem that affected them. We have Amber Alerts and Mothers Against Drunk Driving because someone focused on making meaning out of tragedy. Many people have written their painful stories and testimonies to provide hope and support to those who find themselves in a similar place.

Providing solutions to life's problems is a way to make meaning and give purpose to something that seemed without hope or to help prevent others from experiencing the pain we have felt. We are meaning makers. And one of our greatest strengths as image bearers of God is to find ways to redeem the brokenness around us. This may not take away the grief and sadness we feel, but we add something else to the mix—hope. Hope is the resiliency that allows us to keep going in this big and expansive story we find ourselves in.

Final Note

I know that some of you may be struggling with some pretty heavy circumstances. One of the concerns I have is that it may seem like I've wrapped this study up in a neat, tidy little package that offers little respite from the pain you may be experiencing. I know from working with many people that the ache for things to be good again can be intense and can last for years, sometimes even a lifetime. We are promised that God is familiar with our suffering. I also believe that you can go to Him and pour out all of your pain, anger, sadness, and hurt and He will not reject or abandon you. Jesus Himself cried out to God in anguish, sensing His separation from God on the cross. We feel that way sometimes—like God has turned His back on us, but it isn't so.

My desire is that this study gives you a glimmer of hope amid any painful circumstance you may be going through. I told the story about raising monarch butterflies. I sometimes wonder, if butterflies could speak to their offspring, those caterpillars crawling on their bellies, would they tell them how amazingly different the world is from their perspective above it all? What would those who have gone before us in death tell us if they could from their new perspective?

We have so many limits as humans—we can't see our life's legacy from the grave. We can't see what's around the corner even for tomorrow. We can't see the big picture of how everything works together. We must remember that we experience life from within our personal, limited perspective.

I urge you to have faith that there is more going on than you could ever know, and that you worship a good God who in in charge of everything. He has already written the story and became your personal hero in it through Jesus. If you can hold these truths, maybe you can learn to trust Him even in the most difficult times. If you can seek Him and wait for Him, even when your heart's cry is "Where are you God?", He promises to come near so you can experience some glimpses of Him and His promises to you.

He may answer though His creation, His Word, His people, or however else He chooses to reveal Himself. Maybe then, you can hold on to the hope of what you don't yet have. Maybe, just maybe, you can truly trust that your heart's desire for everything to be as it should be will one day be fulfilled.

Discussion Questions and Reflective Journaling Prompts

Compare who we are in relationship to Adam and to Christ using Romans 5:18–19.

We are currently living in the middle of a complex, emotionally laden adventure story. So much has happened since Eden, but much remains to unfold before the final chapter. How do you see your current challenges in life in light of understanding the grand story we are in?

How has God used your personal story to tell His big story?

Prayer

Dear Lord, You see all and know all. My pain is not foreign to You. You love me and care deeply for me. You came to rescue me, to heal me, to free me, and to save me. Help me to experience Your presence in the midst of suffering. Give me friends and companions that lift me up and demonstrate Your presence and love for me even in suffering. Give me a vision and a hope that all will be made right someday. Wipe the tears from my eyes and lift up my heavy spirit. Let me never forget that You suffered, too, and You understand my suffering. Be my hope and my strength for today and forevermore. Amen

Sources

Daniel DeWitt, "The Difference Between Guilt and Shame," *The Gospel Coalition*, February 19, 2018, https://www.thegospelcoalition.org/article/difference-between-guilt-shame/.

"Fight, Flight, Freeze: What This Response Means," *Healthline*, accessed August 12, 2024, https://www.healthline.com/health/mental-health/fight-flight-freeze.

Kirsten Weir, "Nurtured by Nature: Psychological Research Is Advancing Our Understanding of How Time in Nature Can Improve Our Mental Health and Sharpen Our Cognition," *American Psychological Association* 51, no. 3 (2020): https://www.apa.org/monitor/2020/04/nurtured-nature.

Martin Seligman et al., "Positive Psychology Progress: Empirical Validation of Interventions," *American Psychologist* 60, no. 5 (2005): 410–421, https://doi.org/10.1037/0003-066X.60.5.410.

Y. Joel Wong et al., "Does Gratitude Writing Improve the Mental Health of Psychotherapy Clients?" *Psychotherapy Research*, 28 (2016): 1–11, https://doi.org/10.1080/10503307.2016.1169332.

UNITED STATES OF AMERICA RESOURCES

General Counseling Resources

https://www.goodtherapy.org/find-therapist.html

https://www.psychologytoday.com/us

Christian Counseling

https://nacconline.org/find-a-counselor/

https://aacc.net/

https://www.christiancounselorsnetwork.com

Crisis Hotlines

National Suicide and Crisis Lifeline: 988
For TTY users: Use your preferred relay service or dial 711 then 988.

Alcoholics Anonymous: (212) 870-3400

Childhelp National Child Abuse Hotline: (800) 422-4453

Crisis Text Line: Text HOME to 741741

Acknowledgements

There are some wonderful people who have been a great help to me in completing this project. First, I'd like to thank the Flourish writer's community and especially Mindy Kiker and Jenny Kochert for their help, encouragement and coaching. I'd also like to thank Kathy Brown my editor for her helpful suggestions and polishing up this study and making it sparkle with her amazing editing skills. I'd like to thank Laura H, Wendy K, Stacey P and Debbie B. my book club gals and longtime friends for critiquing this bible study and giving me feedback and enthusiastically supporting me. Thank you to Tod for your continued encouragement and accountability. Thank you to my clients who have entrusted their stories to me as we work together to bring hope, healing and meaning to their lives. Thank you to my parents who pointed me to Jesus at a young age. And thank you to Jesus, my Lord and Savior for pursuing my heart, always helping and healing me and giving me good work to do in this broken but beautiful world.

www.ingramcontent.com/pod-product-compliance
Lightning Source LLC
LaVergne TN
LVHW081325110826
845149LV00007B/1598

* 9 7 9 8 9 9 3 6 5 0 1 0 4 *